PHOTO FUN

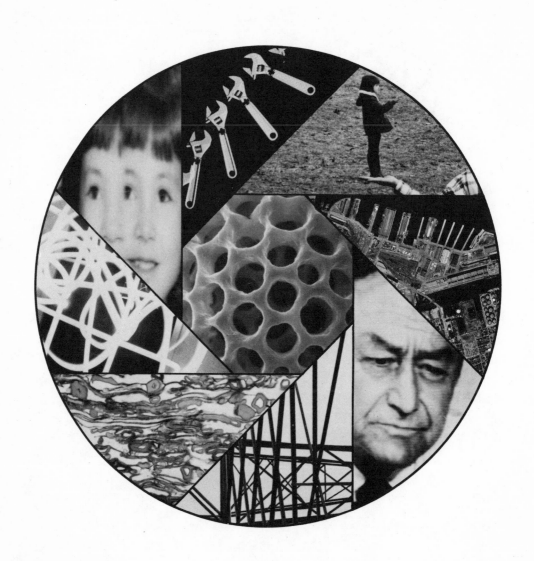

PHOTO FUN

AN IDEA BOOK FOR SHUTTERBUGS

Illustrated with photographs and diagrams

BY DAVID WEBSTER

Franklin Watts, Inc. / New York / 1973

Diagrams by Vantage Art, Inc.

LIBRARY OF CONGRESS CATALOGING IN PUBLICATION DATA

Webster, David, 1930-
   Photo fun.

    SUMMARY: Explains the use of special techniques
and effects in producing unusual photographs.
    1. Photography, Trick–Juvenile literature.
[1. Photography] I. Title.
TR148.W4   778.8   72-8112
ISBN 0-531-02620-5

To my father,
who posed for my
very first photograph
when I was ten.

 **CONTENTS**

# INTRODUCTION

Anyone can be a real photographer. You need not have an expensive camera or your own darkroom. As you become more interested in photography, however, you may want to get better equipment.

I hope this book will give you some ideas for taking what I call "fun photos." The book is not intended to be a manual describing proper camera techniques. The only way to become a good photographer is to take lots of pictures and note what seems to bring the best results. So load your camera and start snapping away.

Have fun!

D.W.

TAKE FUN PHOTOS

Trick pictures . . .

. . . this photo was taken horizontally, with the boy walking on top of a wall. Turn it.

Pictures of small things . . . the sole of a rubber boot, photographed close up.

Pictures from high up . . . a view from an airplane.

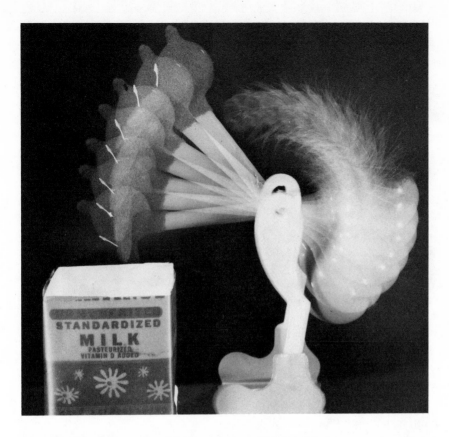

And pictures of moving things . . . a toy dipping bird.

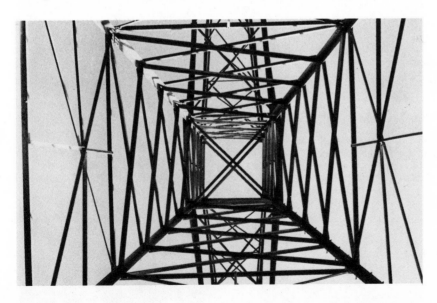

Pictures of familiar things from odd angles . . . a transmission tower, taken from below.

A basketball backstop, taken from underneath.

The end of a smoking-pipe.

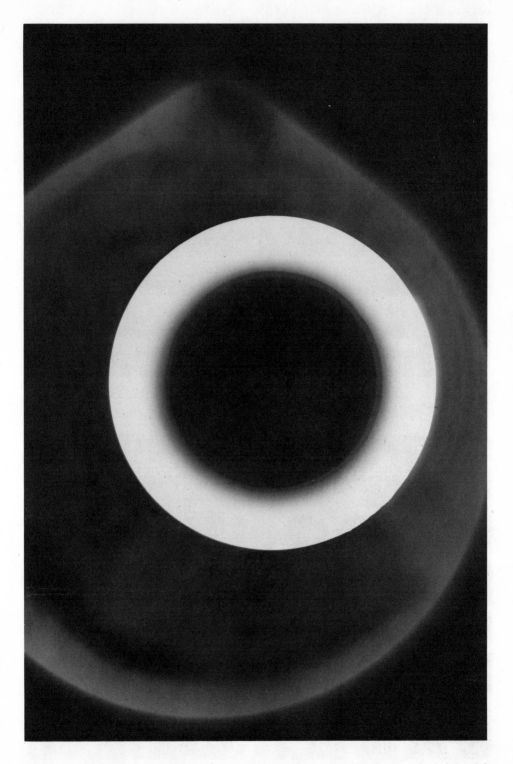

Unusual patterns . . . a photogram made with a glass beaker and a sheet of photographic paper. (See page 80.)

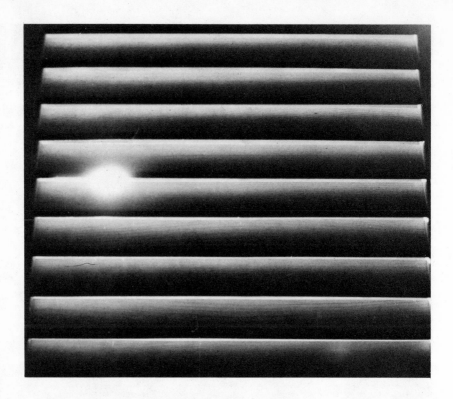

The sun shining through closed Venetian blinds.

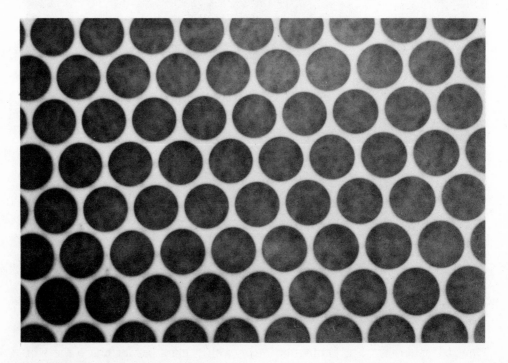

Part of a filter from an oil furnace.

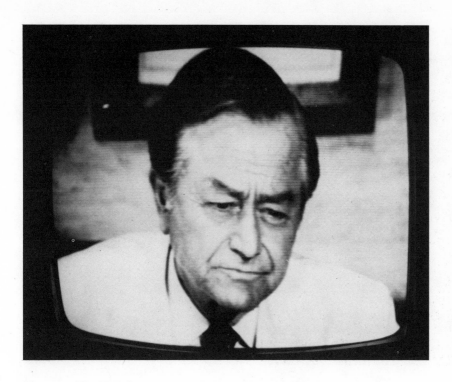

Pictures of a TV show.

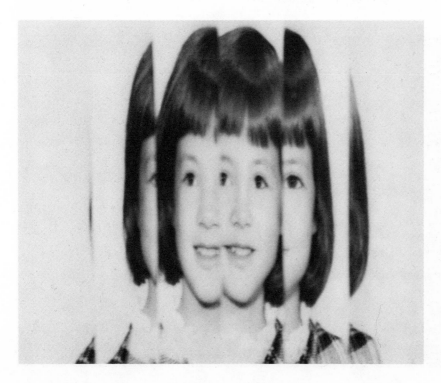

Distortion created by wavy glass. (See page 16.)

Reflections of a flashbulb in animals' eyes.

A triple exposure at night.

Action photos of people . . .

. . . and big fires.

Candid shots — pictures of people who don't know their photos are being taken . . .

 # TRICK PHOTOGRAPHY

The boy, of course, is not holding the two tiny girls. The photo below shows
how the picture was arranged for photographing. You can use this same trick
to get a picture of someone holding up a large tree or an automobile.

Can you figure out how this trick photo and the one on the opposite page were taken?

This is how the boy and the table were placed for the above photograph. The camera was held pointing straight down at the boy.

15

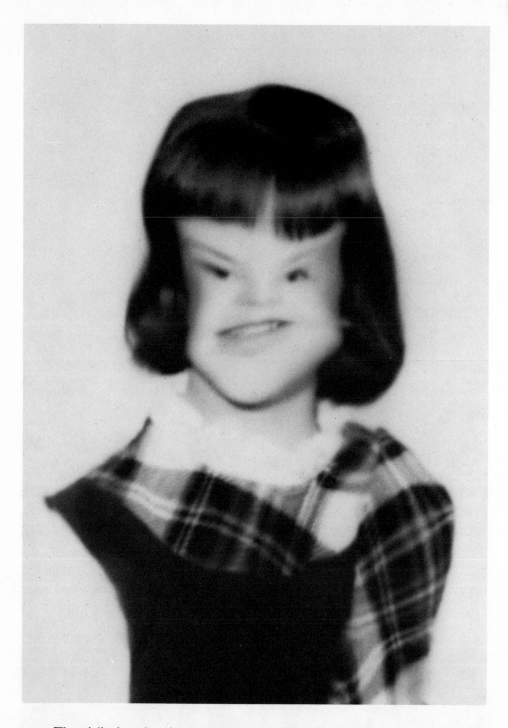

The girl's face has been distorted by holding a piece of wavy glass in front of the camera. Instead of photographing a real person, the portrait shown at the right was used. To get an effect like this, you should have a camera that can focus on an object less than two feet away.

The diagram on the next page shows how to produce distorted pictures. If you do not have a large photograph of someone's face, you can cut a picture from a magazine. Mount the camera on a tripod (see page 30) so that the lens is directly in front of the picture and as close to it as the lens allows. A closeup lens will enable you to position the camera as near as one foot from the picture. The camera should be set at about f/8, with a shutter speed of 1/50 or 1/25 of a second. If the pictures are underexposed, try again, using a slower shutter speed.

Hardware stores often sell wavy pieces of glass that are used in bathroom or front-door windows. The irregular glass allows light in, but is impossible to see through. You could also try a warped piece of thick plastic that has been bent in a warm oven.

DISTORTED PHOTO SET-UP

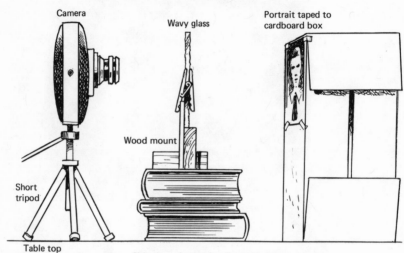

Side view of setup for distorted photo

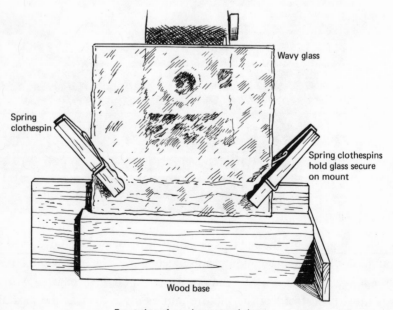

Front view of wood mount and glass

Sometimes double exposures are made by mistake. But you can use a double-exposure technique at night to produce interesting pictures. Use a tripod and make exposures of 5 to 10 seconds with the lens wide open and without advancing the film in the camera.

The lamp seen on the left-hand side of the picture is really far away from the front doorway. One exposure was made of the house door. Then the camera was moved near the lamp and a second exposure was taken on the same film.

In a similar way, you can put a moon in any picture. Photograph the moon when it is in the upper left-hand area of the viewfinder. Then make the second exposure of a house or an outdoor scene at night, leaving a space for the moon in the same corner as in the first exposure.

SPECIAL EFFECTS WITH REFLECTIONS

Store windows are always available to make interesting reflections. The next picture shows how the photograph of the "weirdo" above was taken. The left-hand side of the finished photo is the reflected part.

Here the store window has reflected cars and houses across the street. The stuffed animals and Christmas tree behind the window glass make the photograph look like a double exposure.

One skyscraper is reflected in the windows of another.

Shiny automobiles are good reflectors. This photograph was taken across the roof of a car.

Try taking pictures of reflections in automobile bumpers...

. . . and hubcaps.

Reflections in ponds and lakes are easy to photograph. It is fun to see if people can tell which part of the picture is the reflection in the water. Usually clouds appear more clearly on the water's surface than in the sky.

After a rain, you should be able to shoot reflections in puddles.

With two mirrors you can create a kaleidoscope effect from a portrait. Arrange your equipment as shown below. The angle between the two mirrors must be 60° and can be measured with a protractor. A closeup or portrait lens for the camera is helpful but not necessary. Take a number of different exposures so that at least one will be correct.

KALEIDOSCOPE PHOTO SETUP

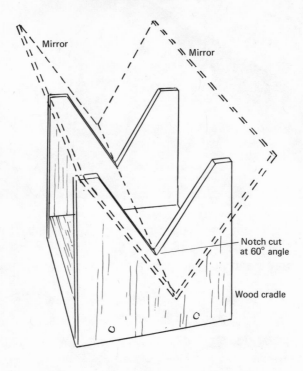

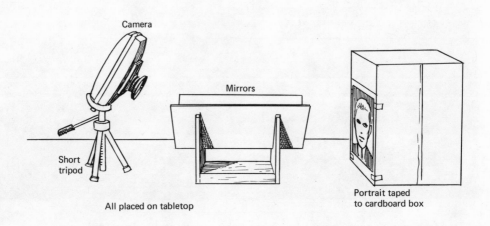

The bright marks in this photograph of the sun were made by sunlight that was reflected from a metal surface inside the camera to the backs of the eight metal blades of the camera's diaphragm, and then back to the film.

TIME EXPOSURES AT NIGHT

A time exposure is a photograph taken with the camera lens open for a long time. Usually, when you take a snapshot, the shutter opens for only a fraction of a second, so a shutter speed of 1 second is a long time. Sometimes a time exposure can take many minutes, or even hours.

The two photos below are time exposures. Can you figure out how they were taken?

Many cameras have a setting that allows the shutter to remain open as long as desired. Cameras that are less expensive, though, have no time-exposure setting. You can still take time exposures with these cameras by holding the shutter open with a piece of tape. Open the back of your camera and find the two or three little screws inside (see sketch opposite). Remove the screws with a small screwdriver, and the front of the camera should come off. Now you can see what happens inside when you push the shutter lever to take a picture. Turn the film sprocket to release the shutter each time you click it.

Use a small piece of masking tape to hold the shutter open. Then replace the front of the camera by screwing it on again.

Of course, you should not place film in a camera while the shutter is open, so you will have to make another "shutter" on the outside of the lens. A disc cut from stiff black paper can be taped over the lens. Be sure it fits tightly, or light will leak in and ruin the film. To take a time exposure, merely remove the black paper for as long as you want. Cover the lens again before winding the film to the next number.

THREE STEPS FOR CONVERTING INSTAMATIC CAMERA

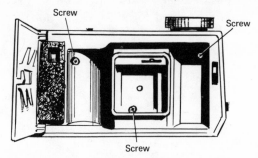

1. Remove small screws inside camera

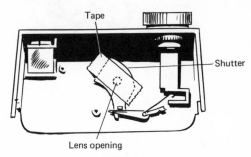

2. Tape shutter open

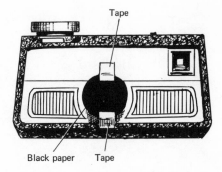

3. Cover front of lens with black paper disc

It is essential that your camera be held perfectly still when you take a time exposure. If the camera moves while the lens is open, your picture will be blurry.

A tripod is the best way to mount a camera so that it does not move.

Tripods can be purchased at a camera store at prices from five to twenty-five dollars. Most cameras have a threaded hole for attaching the tripod screw. If your camera does not have such a hole, you cannot use a tripod. Even if your camera can be attached to a regular tripod, you may want to make your own mount in order to save money.

The sketches below show how to build a homemade camera holder from wood. Make two L-shaped brackets from four strips of wood. To keep each bracket from coming loose, both pieces should either be screwed together or glued and nailed. The two brackets are joined together with a bolt and wing nut through holes in the wood.

Attach your camera to one of the brackets. Use a short bolt in the special tripod hole, or just tape the camera to the wooden strip at either end.

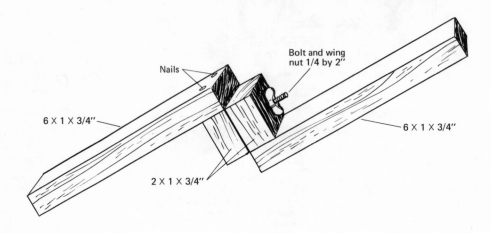

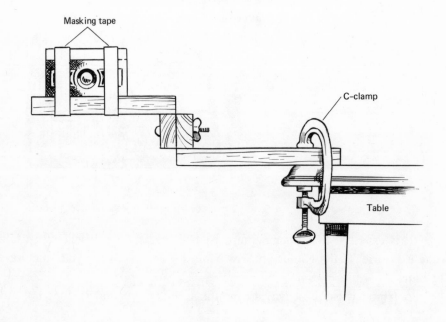

The other bracket can be secured to a chair or tabletop with a small C-clamp. The camera is aimed up or down by loosening the wing nut.

When you take a picture, push down on the shutter lever slowly, so that you do not shake the camera. Most cameras have a place for attaching a cable release — a flexible wire that moves within a sheath and trips your camera shutter. If you use one of these, there is less chance of wiggling the camera. The cable release should have a screw to lock the shutter open when you let go.

Time exposures are often used to take pictures where there is not enough light for an ordinary snapshot. The inside of your house is a good example. While there is enough light for your eyes to see, it is usually too dark for the camera to take a regular picture without a flashbulb. To get more light on the film without a flashbulb, the lens has to be open for a longer period of time.

It is difficult to know just how long an exposure should be. The time depends upon the size of the camera's diaphragm opening, the type of film, and the amount of light in the room. To take a good time exposure, you must experiment by taking a series of exposures of different lengths. You could use a one-second exposure for the first picture. Then take others with exposures of 2 seconds, 5 seconds, and 10 seconds. Be sure to write down what you do each time, to remind you when the film is returned from being printed. Developed negatives have tiny numbers at the bottom to show in what order the pictures were taken.

Try taking some pictures inside the house during the day, and others at night with the lights on.

Photographers often keep a record of each picture they take. In the table on the next page, notice the different information that has been recorded. The check marks indicate which exposures were best. The next time the photographer wants to take a similar picture, he can refer to the table and know just how to set his camera.

1 second   *2 seconds*   *5 seconds*   *10 seconds*   *15 seconds*

Which amount of time gave the best exposure?

MODEL EXPOSURE CHART

Subject	Diaphragm opening	Time	Type of film	Best exposure
	2	15 min	Tri-X	
	2	5 min	Tri-X	
	2	1 min	Tri-X	✓
	2	1/2 sec	Tri-X	
	2	10 sec	Tri-X	
	2	1 min	Tri-X	
	2	1/2 min	Tri-X	
	2	10 sec	Tri-X	
	4.5	1/2 min	Tri-X	✓
	4.5	10 sec	Tri-X	
	2	1/10 sec	Pan-X	
	2	1/5 sec	Pan-X	
	2	1/2 sec	Pan-X	
	2	1 sec	Pan-X	✓
	2	2 sec	Pan-X	

A picture taken with a flashbulb is exposed correctly only at a distance of from several feet to about 10 feet. Objects very close to the camera are too light; things farther away than 10 feet are too dark. A properly exposed time photo is evenly lighted all over.

This is an over-exposed flash photo.

This is a properly exposed time exposure.

What is wrong with these time exposures?

When photographing lighted buildings at night, you need only a short exposure of about one second.

The fire was bright enough to be photographed at 1/10 of a second.

You can also take time exposures outside by moonlight. Wait until there is a full moon. Clamp your camera mount to a wooden desk chair and carry it outside. Since the moon is not very bright, your exposure must be quite long. Try 1 minute, 5 minutes, and 15 minutes. Which is the best exposure time?

The stars give off even less light than the moon. But they are still bright enough to show up on film. Since the earth is spinning, the stars appear to move continually in the sky. The bright lines made on film by stars are known as "star tracks."

Take star photos on a clear night when there is no moon. Lay your camera on the ground, pointed into the sky. Use exposures from a few minutes to several hours.

About how long was this exposure? Remember stars appear to make a complete revolution around the polestar every twenty-four hours.

Why are some star tracks curved and others almost straight? As you probably know, the earth rotates on its axis. The North Star, or polestar, is almost directly over the North Pole. All stars appear to turn in a counter-clockwise direction around the North Star. The closer a star is to the North Star, the more its path is curved.

On color film the star tracks show up in different colors. The color of a star is caused by its temperature; most blue stars and white stars are hotter than yellow stars and red ones. To the eye, almost all stars look plain white.

Here a shooting star has crossed the paths of other stars. The only way to get such a picture is by being lucky.

You can use a flashlight to make tracks of light on film. At night, turn off all the lights inside your house. Have someone stand about 20 feet away and wave a flashlight around while it is pointed at a mounted camera with an open lens. In this way you can make a design, a drawing, or even your name.

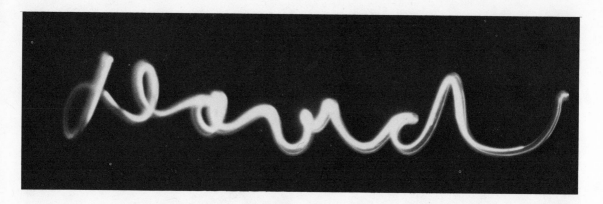

A more symmetrical pattern can be made with a flashlight pendulum. Hang a flashlight on a string so that it is 6 or 8 feet above the ground. You will probably have to use a tree branch outside at night to get high enough. Start the light swinging and open the shutter for about 15 seconds.

A simple pendulum can make only circular or elliptical paths. More interesting patterns can be obtained from a compound pendulum made with two strings as illustrated on the next page. Change the length of the strings after each exposure in order to get different effects.

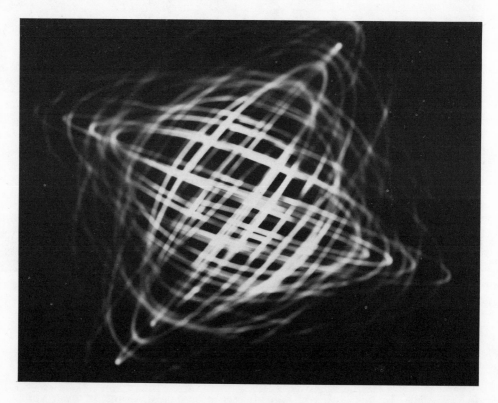

This is a compound pendulum pattern.

COMPOUND PENDULUM SET-UP

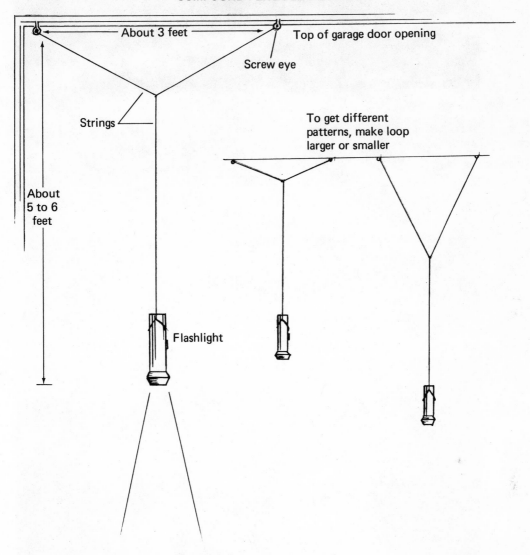

About 3 feet

Top of garage door opening

Screw eye

Strings

To get different patterns, make loop larger or smaller

About 5 to 6 feet

Flashlight

Camera

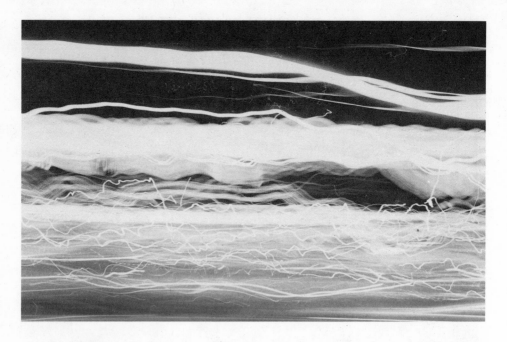

Another way to get light patterns is to take a time exposure while driving through a city at night. Open the camera lens for 5 to 15 seconds as your car goes past lighted signs or buildings.

You can also photograph cars as they travel down the road at night. Their headlights and taillights make bright streaks on the film. What would this kind of picture look like in color?

This lightning occurred in a thunderstorm caused by a volcanic eruption in Iceland. The exposure was for 90 seconds.

Aerial bursts at a fireworks display look even better in color.

Lights can be made starlike on film if two pieces of window screen are held in front of the lens. The screening should be crossed at an angle of about 45°.

PHOTOS OF FAST THINGS

In order to "stop" action on film, you need to use a fast shutter speed. 1/100 of a second will give a clear picture of people walking. An even faster shutter speed might be necessary to "freeze" racing cars, skiers, or breaking waves. This ice hockey action was taken at 1/250 of a second.

Often a partly blurred photograph is more interesting. The fuzzy hands and feet of the running boys above give an impression of speed. In the next picture, notice that only the cars close to the camera are blurred.

"Panning" is another technique for photographing fast things. To pan a skier, for example, you look through the viewfinder and smoothly move the camera to follow the action. When the skier passes by, snap the picture. The blurry background adds to the feeling of motion.

Multiple-exposure photographs are usually made with a strobe light, a device that makes a rapid series of bright flashes. The wrench in the next photo was mounted so that it would spin slowly as it traveled along a track. The shutter of the camera was opened, and a picture was taken every time the strobe flashed.

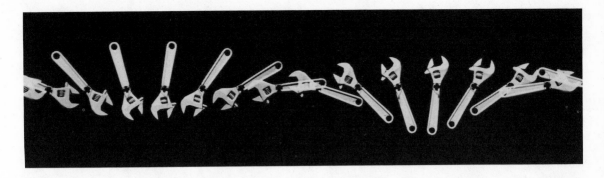

You can make a gadget to get a strobe effect with flashbulbs. The photograph below of the girl walking was taken with six flashbulbs discharged in the simple homemade device described on the next page.

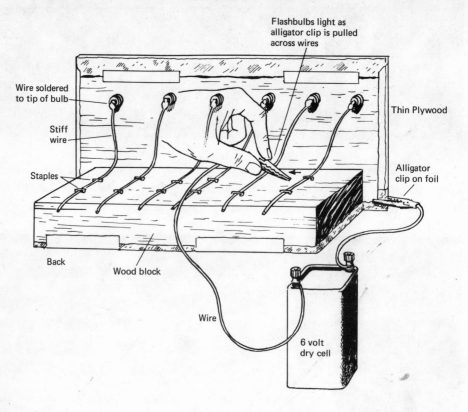

Flashbulbs light as alligator clip is pulled across wires

Wire soldered to tip of bulb

Stiff wire

Staples

Back

Wood block

Wire

Thin Plywood

Alligator clip on foil

6 volt dry cell

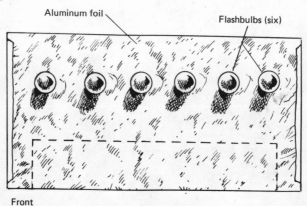

Aluminum foil

Flashbulbs (six)

Front

When the free wire from the battery is drawn across the wires on the board, the bulbs will flash in quick succession. The camera should be mounted on a tripod, and the lens must remain open as the exposures are made.

There can be no background behind the subject being photographed. The easiest way to achieve this is to set up outside at night. Keep away from trees and buildings.

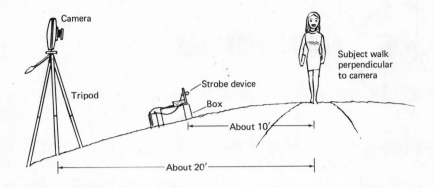

The single flash of a strobe light is required to photograph very fast motion. Here a rifle bullet has just passed through a light bulb.

6 AERIAL PICTURES

Aerial photographs are usually taken from an airplane. But you can get good aerial pictures without flying. One way is to use a tall tree or a high building. The picture below of the children was taken from the second-floor window of their school.

In cities, skyscrapers provide fine vantage points for photographing other buildings.

This picture was taken by a remote camera, from the top of the school flagpole. The shutter was depressed by an electrical plunger called a solenoid. You should be able to buy a 6-volt, plunger-type solenoid from a large electrical store for about $10. The apparatus can be assembled as shown on the next page.

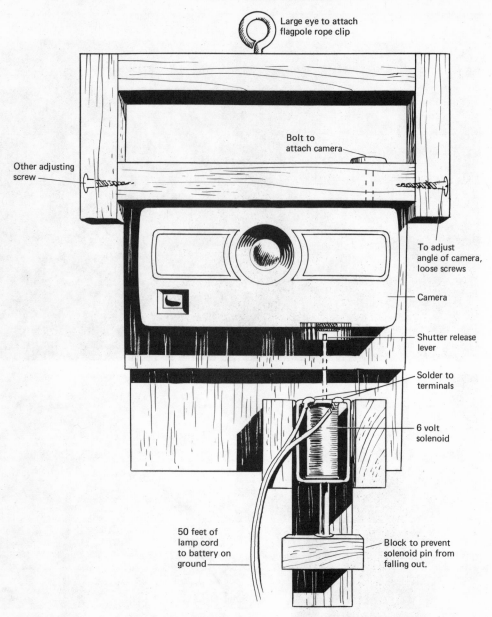

Large eye to attach flagpole rope clip

Bolt to attach camera

Other adjusting screw

To adjust angle of camera, loose screws

Camera

Shutter release lever

Solder to terminals

6 volt solenoid

50 feet of lamp cord to battery on ground

Block to prevent solenoid pin from falling out.

When the wire is touched to the battery, the solenoid plunger snaps out and takes a picture. Of course, you should get permission before you use any flagpole. Most public buildings, such as schools, libraries, town halls, and fire stations, have poles that you could use to hoist a camera aloft.

Ever since cameras were invented, men have devised ways to take photographs from the sky. The first aerial photo was taken in 1858 from a manned balloon 262 feet above Paris. Only a few years later, two British balloonists took pictures from a huge balloon that rose several miles high. By 1910, cameras had been lifted high into the air by kites, rockets, airplanes, and even pigeons.

Of these methods, a kite-borne camera is the only one feasible for you to attempt. The kite camera should have a solenoid arrangement similar to that used for the flagpole picture. A lighter holder can be made from a strip of aluminum sold in hardware stores. The sketch shows how the holder is bent. An inexpensive camera should be used, since there is a danger of the camera being lost or damaged. Also, a plastic camera is much lighter than a metal one.

SOLENOID HOLDER FOR KITE CAMERA

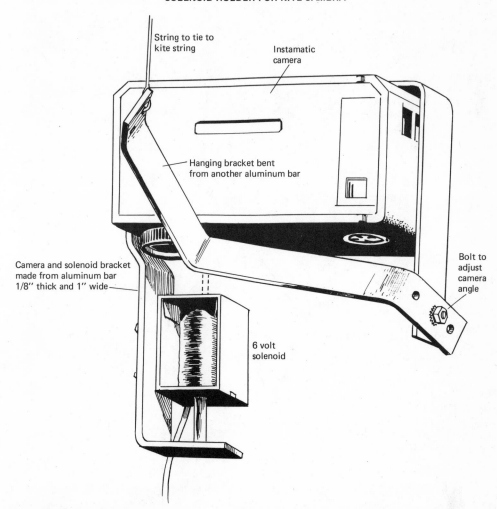

String to tie to kite string

Instamatic camera

Hanging bracket bent from another aluminum bar

Camera and solenoid bracket made from aluminum bar 1/8" thick and 1" wide

Bolt to adjust camera angle

6 volt solenoid

Several paper box kites are the best for carrying a camera into the air. You will need a fairly windy day. Use a good nylon string to launch the first kite. When the kite is about 50 feet high, fly a second kite on a short piece of string, and tie it to the main string. Use a double loop knot so that the kite stays in place. Depending upon the wind's strength, a series of two to four kites will be needed to lift the camera and wires.

Hang the camera about 50 feet below the bottom kite and adjust its angle so that the lens points toward the ground. Attach a long length of insulated, two-strand wire to the solenoid. A 12-volt car battery is a good source of electricity for the 6-volt solenoid.

BOX KITES LIFTING CAMERA

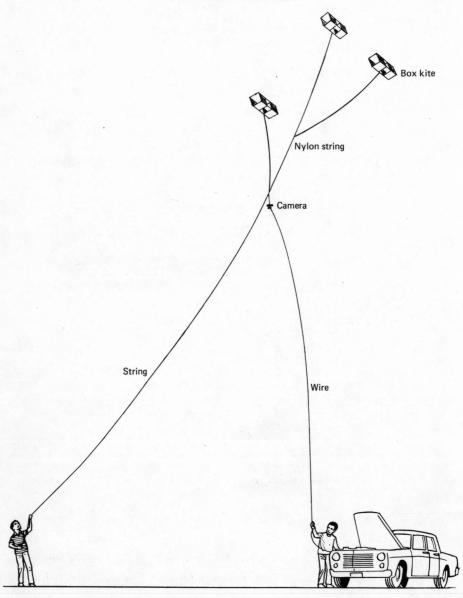

Box kite

Nylon string

Camera

String

Wire

Let out more string until the camera is as high as the wire allows. Touch the wires to the battery terminals to take your aerial photograph. Of course, to get another picture you must pull down the camera and advance the film.

The development of aerial photography has greatly simplified mapping techniques. This is an aerial view of a section of Boston, Massachusetts.

A special wide-angle lens was used to take this photograph of New York City.

The farmlands of Wisconsin form interesting patterns from the air. In these fields, crops have been planted in strips that follow the contours of the land.

An infrared scanner can photograph heat to make a "thermal print." This heat photo shows where a power plant is discharging hot wastes into the Connecticut River.

This view of the rising earth greeted the Apollo 8 astronauts as they came from behind the moon after their lunar-orbit insertion burn.

CAMERA "TRAPS" FOR ANIMALS

It is difficult to take photographs of most wild animals because they are afraid of you. Before you can get close enough to a squirrel to take its picture, it scampers away up a tree. One way to photograph such timid creatures, however, is with a *remote* camera release. This will allow you to operate your camera while you hide some distance away.

Your camera will need a firm support so that it will not move when you pull the string. If the camera has a tripod socket, you can bolt it to a piece of wood with a ¼ by 20 bolt. Cameras without a bolt hole can be secured with tape.

The simplest type of release is merely a string attached to the lever that releases the camera's shutter. The direction of pull is changed by running the string through screw eyes.

STRING PULL FOR LEVER-TYPE SHUTTER RELEASE

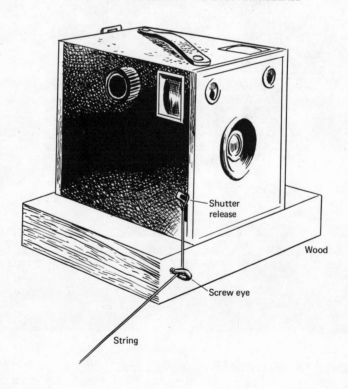

Shutter release

Wood

Screw eye

String

Many cameras have a plunger-type shutter release. If you have this type of camera, you can make a lever arrangement to depress the plunger. The shorter end of the lever should be positioned over the plunger to increase the force of your pull on the string.

STRING PULL FOR PLUNGER–TYPE SHUTTER RELEASE

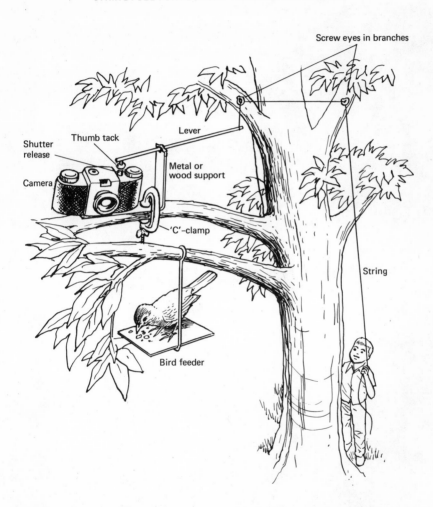

Even with a string release, you cannot photograph animals unless you locate your camera in the right place. Bait can be put out to attract game to come close to the camera. Birds can often be photographed at a feeder or birdbath.

No matter where you put the camera, you may have to wait a long time for an animal to come. You can avoid wasting time by using an *automatic* remote release. The plans on page 65 show one way to make a "trap" that will photograph animals in your absence.

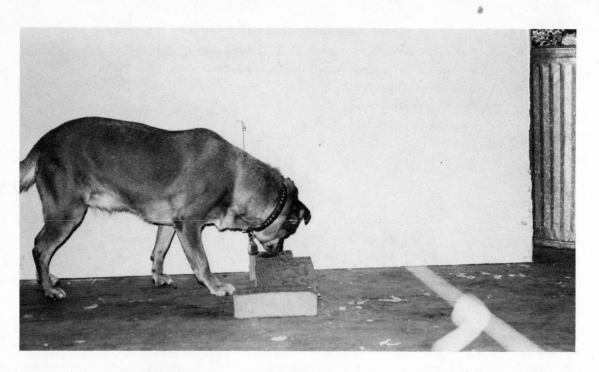

This dog was "caught" inside the author's garage where the garbage cans were frequently raided by unknown animals at night.

Sometimes your trap may be set off accidentally by a two-legged animal.

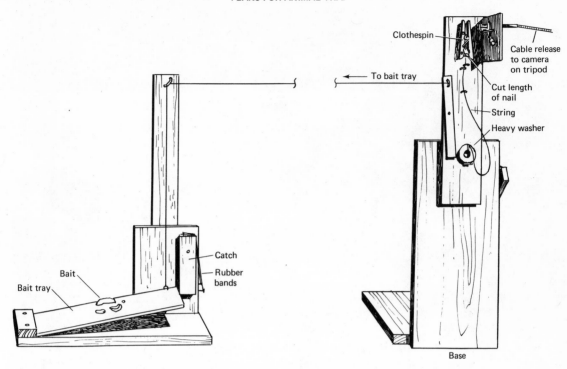

More expensive cameras can be fitted with a cable release, as shown. A spring clothespin can then be mounted so that it will depress the cable plunger when in the closed position. The jaws of the clothespin can be propped open with a short nail attached to a long string. When the animal begins to eat the bait, the wooden tray falls and pulls the string. The nail is pulled from the clothespin, which springs closed to snap a picture.

For animals that come out only at night, your camera must have a flash attachment. Also, if the camera is placed outdoors, it needs a cover for protection against rain. Of course, after one picture has been taken, you must advance the film, change the flashbulb, and reset the "trap." Check the camera occasionally to see if it needs to be reset.

With a solenoid, you can rig up an automatic animal "trap" much more easily. The solenoid can be connected to the shutter release in the manner shown on page 54. Instead of connecting the battery by hand, though, you can construct an automatic switch. Two simple designs are explained on the next page.

The mousetrap switch can be connected to a string stretched near the bait. If an animal touches the string, the mousetrap should snap shut. When electricity from the battery activates the solenoid, a picture is taken. The bell is connected in the circuit to signal when the trap has sprung, since the battery will run down if not disconnected.

PLANS FOR MOUSE TRAP SWITCH

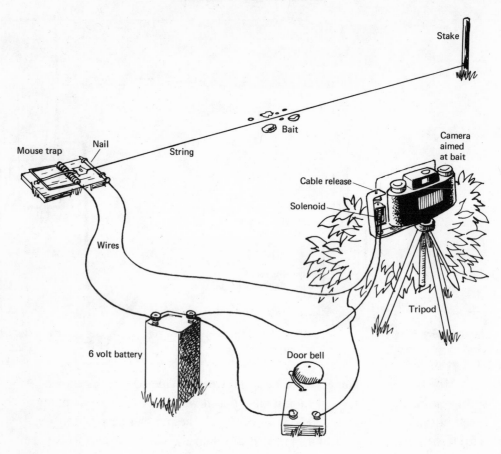

Stake

Bait

Camera aimed at bait

Nail

Mouse trap

String

Cable release

Solenoid

Wires

Tripod

6 volt battery

Door bell

PLANS FOR TREADLE SWITCH

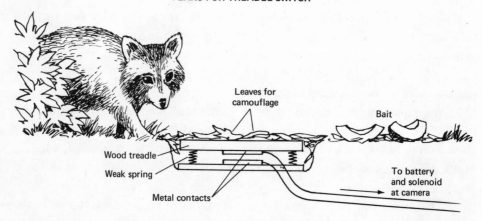

Leaves for camouflage

Bait

Wood treadle

Weak spring

Metal contacts

To battery and solenoid at camera

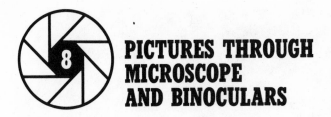

PICTURES THROUGH MICROSCOPE AND BINOCULARS

Familiar objects often look quite unfamiliar when seen at larger than their normal size. The close-up below is a row of staples and the following one is a soda cracker. The pictures were taken with a camera that had a removable lens. By placing rings between the back of the camera and the lens, the camera can be made to focus on objects a few inches away.

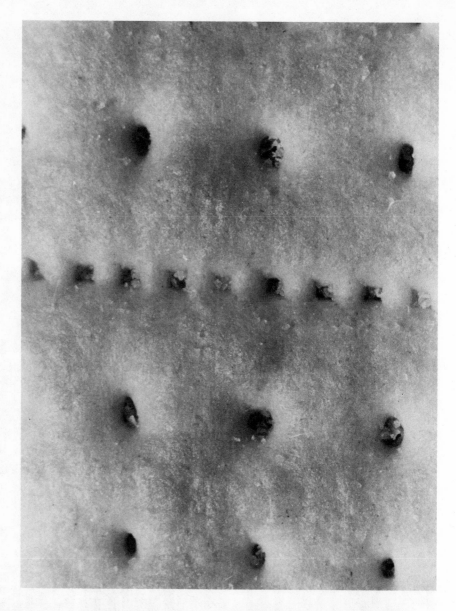

You can take photographs through a microscope with almost any camera. The camera must be mounted over the microscope as shown on page 70. To obtain proper focus, turn on the projector's lamp so that the light shines on the mirror and up through the microscope tube. Hold a sheet of paper above the eyepiece and move the paper slowly up and down to find where the spot of light is the smallest. The camera lens should be positioned at this point. Before moving the microscope into position, focus it with low power on a good slide. Set the camera on infinity, open the diaphragm fully, and try exposures of 1/100 and 1/50 of a second. The next photo is of a fly wing through a microscope.

A scanning electron microscope can magnify as much as 100,000 times. The edge of a sheet of paper is enlarged here 125 times.

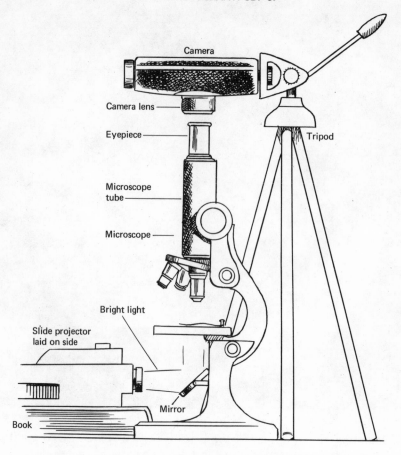

Camera

Camera lens

Eyepiece

Microscope
tube

Microscope

Tripod

Bright light

Slide projector
laid on side

Mirror

Book

Here fossilized diatoms — plant microorganisms — are magnified 1,000 times.

This photo of a cupola was taken through a pair of binoculars. Photographed from the same place, without the binoculars, the cupola almost disappears.

Of course, the best way to take telephotos — photos of distant objects — is with a telephoto lens. But special lenses are quite expensive and are not made to fit many cameras. The plans below show how a pair of binoculars can be mounted as a substitute for a telephoto lens.

A small hand telescope is not suitable for taking telephotos. This is because, once the telescope is in position, there is no way to aim it accurately at your subject. With binoculars, you can peer through one eyepiece while the camera lens is behind the second eyepiece.

Focusing is no problem with a reflex camera, which has a ground-glass plate showing how the picture will appear on the film. With most cameras, though, the only way to obtain a sharp photograph is to focus on a piece of waxed paper before the film is inserted into the camera. Open the camera so that you can see the space where the film passes behind the lens. Cut a strip of waxed paper the same width as the film, and tape it in the film slot. Be sure the paper is flat and is in the same space that the film occupies.

To hold the camera steady, rest it on some convenient object such as the hood of a car or a fence post. Now set the camera lens at infinity and focus the binoculars until a clear picture appears on the waxed paper. Keep your eyes about six inches behind the camera. You will be able to view the image on the waxed paper more easily if you darken the space behind the camera by draping a coat over your head and the camera.

When your focusing adjustments are complete, remove the waxed paper and insert the film. The shutter speed and lens opening should be set as usual. Take a few shots without changing the adjustment of the binoculars. Then try others after moving the focusing knob slightly one way and then the other.

SET-UP FOR PHOTOGRAPHING THROUGH BINOCULARS

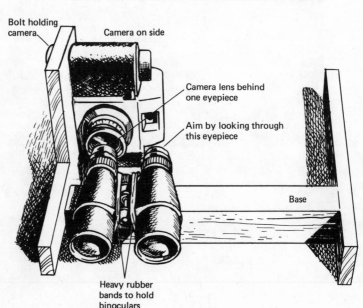

Bolt holding camera

Camera on side

Camera lens behind one eyepiece

Aim by looking through this eyepiece

Base

Heavy rubber bands to hold binoculars

A giant spiral galaxy has been photographed here through a large telescope.

UNDERWATER PICTURES

When taking underwater pictures from above the water, it is important to use some sort of clear viewing container. This can be merely a glass baking dish or a clear plastic tray. The water viewer allows you to take photographs through a perfectly smooth material rather than the usual wavy or rippling water surface. Float the viewer on the water and hold the camera just above it when taking a picture. Since there is always less light underwater, you must use a wider lens opening or a longer shutter speed.

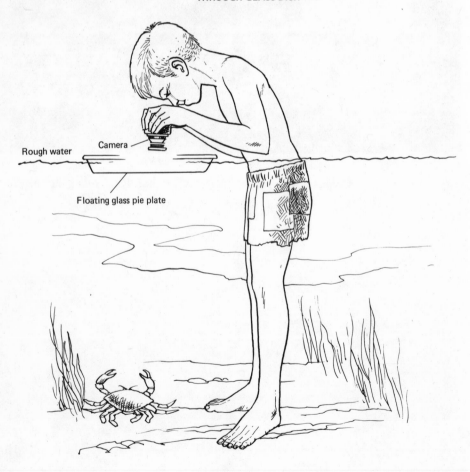

**TAKING PHOTO INTO WATER
THROUGH GLASS DISH**

Rough water

Camera

Floating glass pie plate

Tidepools show up best when lighted by the sun.

This tidepool picture was taken without a water viewer. Notice how much less you can see on the bottom.

The next time you go swimming, take along your camera. Of course, you will need to enclose the camera in a large plastic bag to keep it dry. To prevent the water pressure from forcing the plastic against the lens, you must cover the front of the camera with a piece of glass or stiff plastic. You could use the lens from a flashlight or even a swim mask. If the stiff plastic is small, it should be taped over the lens. Put the camera into the bag and secure the top with several tight rubber bands.

You can adjust the camera settings while it is inside the bag. Use different exposures so your pictures are not underexposed in the dark water. Objects under water appear closer than they really are. For this reason, if you are photographing something 4 feet away, the camera distance should be set at 3 feet. Move the camera inside the bag until the lens is covered by a single layer of plastic. You can take the picture by pressing on the bag where it touches the shutter release.

CAMERA IN PLASTIC BAG FOR UNDERWATER PHOTOGRAPHY

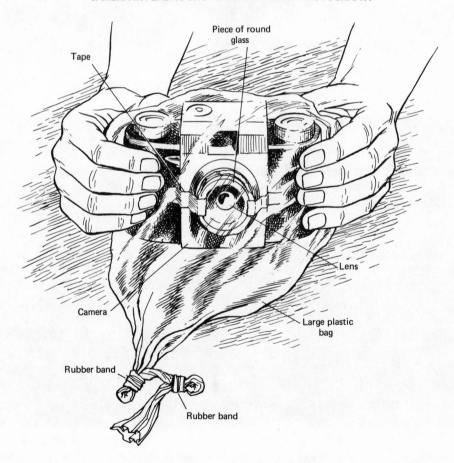

Probably the greatest difficulty with underwater photography is dirty water. You might have the best luck in clear swimming pool water. In a lake or pond you should take pictures only of nearby objects. Even water that looks clear often contains floating dirt particles which scatter the light and make photographs look foggy. For the best results, aim your camera somewhat toward the bottom.

The frogman is working on the Nemo capsule as it breaks water after a test dive.

This strange animal, an umbellula, about three feet tall, was photographed by chance three miles beneath the Atlantic Ocean.

PICTURES WITHOUT CAMERAS

"Odds and Ends."

"Flowers."

The pictures on the previous page were made without any camera. While in the dark, different objects were placed on photographic printing paper. A bright light was then turned on for a few seconds. When the light-sensitive paper was developed, those parts of the paper that were shaded by the objects remained white.

You can make such "photograms" with a studio proof paper bought from a camera store. Unlike most photo-printing paper, studio proof paper is not immediately exposed when opened in the light. Place one sheet, shiny side up, on a large book or a piece of cardboard. Then put some interesting objects on the paper and carry the whole thing outdoors into the sunlight. Soon you should see the paper change from white to dark red. A bright light indoors will work the same as sunlight, but it takes a little longer. Take the objects from the paper only after removing it from the bright light. Now you have a photogram.

PHOTOGRAM TECHNIQUE

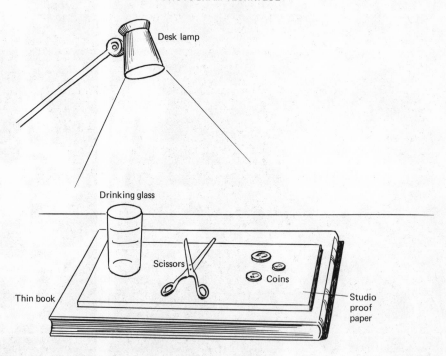

Of course, the white areas in the photogram will slowly continue to change color even in the dimmer room light. To prevent this from happening, the photogram needs to be "fixed" in *hypo*. This chemical is available in photo supply stores. Mix the liquid as directed and pour some into a tray. If a photogram is dipped into hypo for a few minutes, it will no longer be light sensitive.

After dipping, wash it in running water for 10 to 15 minutes and allow it to dry. To flatten out the paper after drying, press it under heavy books for a few days.

DIPPING, DRYING, & PRESSING PHOTOGRAM

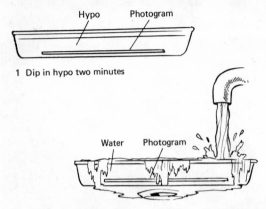

Hypo   Photogram

1 Dip in hypo two minutes

Water   Photogram

2 Wash in running water 10 to 15 minutes

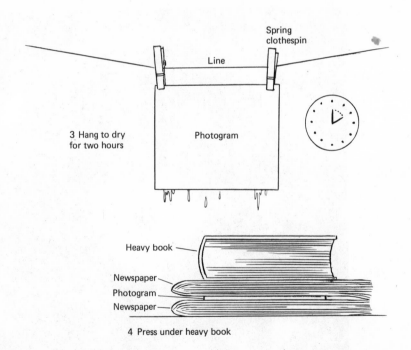

Spring
clothespin

Line

3 Hang to dry
for two hours

Photogram

Heavy book

Newspaper
Photogram
Newspaper

4 Press under heavy book

Photograms can be made with regular photographic paper in a photo darkroom, but special chemicals are required for developing. Blueprint paper can also be used; only water is required to develop the paper after its exposure to light.

What objects were used to make these photograms?

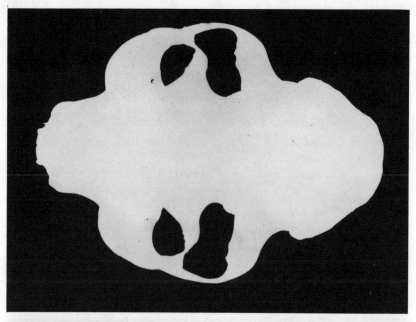

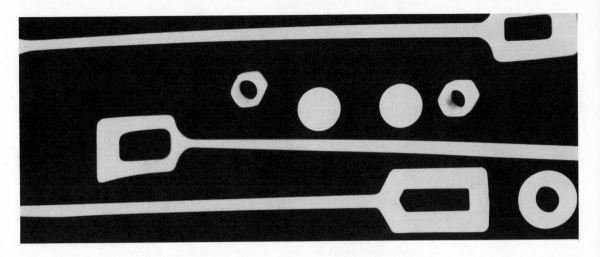

The picture below of light refracting around a razor blade was taken by Richard Livingston of Bayside, New York. Here is his description of how he took it.

The picture was taken by having a small light bulb on the floor next to the wall of my darkroom. The razor blade was stuck in an eraser in the middle of the room, and the film (Tri-X) was at the far end of the room in a film holder. To provide "monochromatic light," I had a red filter in front of the light bulb. The separation between the light and the knife [razor blade] and the film was about two yards. The exposure was for fifteen minutes.

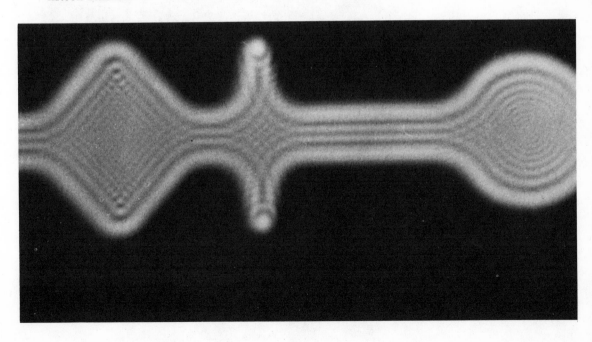

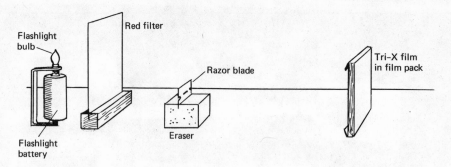

You can be creative with photograms and by **using** simple household items, actually "draw pictures" such as the one below entitled "The Java."

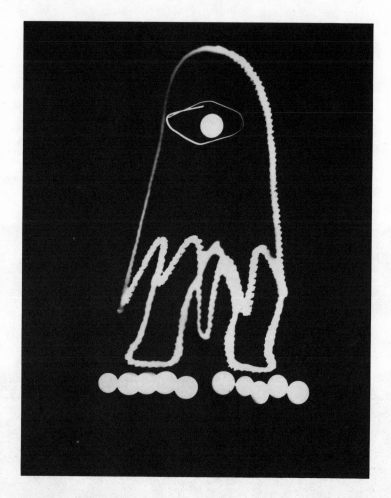

Photo Credits

Richard Iwema top p. 4, p. 67, p. 68; *Bruce Wells* bottom p. 4; *Education Development Center from* PSSC Physics, *D. C. Heath and Company, Lexington, Massachusetts, 1965* top p. 5; *George Tinder* bottom, p. 5; *Jim Butzbach* top p. 6; *Karl Franzen* bottom p. 6; *Robert Radest* p. 7; *Matt Draper* top p. 8; *Brian Knedler* bottom p. 8; *Pam Hughes* top p. 10; *Douglas Seager, Education Development Center* bottom p. 27; *Doug Webster* top p. 33; *Yerkes Observatory* p. 38, p. 73; *James W. Young, Jet Propulsion Laboratory, Table Mountain Observatory* p. 39; *Sigurgeir Johasson, from* Raindrops and Volcanoes *by Duncan Blanchard, c 1966, 1967 by Doubleday & Co., Inc. Reproduced by permission of the publisher* p. 43; *Ned Finkel* p. 44; *Reproduced by permission of Elementary Science Study, Education Development Center, Newton, Massachusetts* top p. 49; *H. E. Edgerton* p. 51; *New England Survey Services, Inc.* p. 57; *United States Coast and Geodetic Survey* p. 58; *United States Department of Agriculture* p. 59; *Coastal Research Corporation* p. 60; *National Aeronautics and Space Administration* p. 61; *Forest Products Laboratory, U.S. Forest Service* bottom p. 69; *Robert Ogilvie, Electron Optics Laboratory, Massachusetts Institute of Technology* p. 70; *United States Navy* p. 77; *United States Naval Oceanographic Office* p. 78; *David Dix* left p. 79; *Paula Aylward* right p. 79; *Tad Costanis* top p. 82; *Sasha Harrison* bottom p. 82; *Marilyn Nutting* top p. 83; *Richard Livingston* bottom p. 83; *Walter Greeley* p. 84.

 **INDEX**

 **About the Author**

David Webster is a former elementary and junior high school science teacher and served for four years as director of science for the Lincoln, Massachusetts, school system. He is now a science consultant for the Wellesley public schools, and has written numerous science-activity articles for children's magazines. His latest Franklin Watts book *Track Watching* was selected as an honor book by the New York Academy of Science.

A man of boundless energy and imagination, Mr. Webster is co-owner and co-director of Camp Netop, a boys' camp in Maine, and he has been a Boy Scout leader for many years. He and his family live in Lincoln, Massachusetts.